MESSAGE FROM THE PRESIDENT OF THE UNITED STATES.

———•◦•———

To the House of Representatives :

In answer to the resolution of the House of Representatives of January 25th, I have the honor to submit the following, accompanied by the report of the Attorney-General, to whom the resolution was referred : Representations having been made to me that in certain portions of South Carolina a condition of lawlessness and terror exists, I requested the then Attorney-General (Akerman) to visit the State, and after a personal examination to report to me the facts in relation to the subject. On the 16th of October last he addressed a communication from South Carolina, in which he stated that in the counties of Spartanburg, York, Chester, Union, Laurens, Newbury, Fairfield, Lancaster and Chesterfield there were combinations for the purpose of preventing the free political action of citizens who were friendly to the Constitution and the Government of the United States, and of depriving the emancipated class of 'the equal protection of the laws. These combinations embrace al least two-thirds of the active white men of those counties and have the sympathy and countenance of a

majority of the other third. They are connected with
similar combinations in other counties and States,
and are no doubt a part of a grand system of criminal
associations pervading most of the Southern States.
The members are bound to obedience and secrecy
by oaths which they are taught to regard as of a
higher obligation than the lawful oath taken before
civil magistrates. They are organized and armed.
They effect their objects by personal violence, often
extending to murder. They terrify witnesses, they
control juries in the State courts, and sometimes in
the courts of the United States. Systematic spying
is one of the means by which the prosecution of the
members is defeated. From information given by
officers of the State and of the United States, and by
credible private citizens, I am justified in affirming
that the instances of criminal violence perpetrated by
these combinations within the last twelve months, in
the above named counties, could be reckoned by
thousands. I received information of a similar import
from various sources, among which were the Joint
Committee of Congress upon Southern Outrages, the
officers of the State, the military officers of the United
States on duty in South Carolina, the United States
Attorney and Marshal, and other officers of the Government, repentant and abjuring members of those
unlawful organizations, persons specially employed
by the Department of Justice to detect crimes against

the United States, and from other credible sources. Most, if not all of this information, except what I derived from the Attorney-General, came to me orally, and was to the effect that the said counties were under the sway of powerful combinations, popularly known as the Ku-Klux Klan, the objects of which are, by force and terror, to prevent all political action not in accord with the views of the members, to deprive colored citizens of the right to bear arms, and of the right of a free ballot, to suppress the schools in which colored children were taught, and to reduce the colored people to a condition closely allied to that of slavery; that these combinations were organized and armed, and had rendered the local law ineffectual to protect the classes whom they desired to oppress; that they had perpetrated many murders, and hundreds of crimes of minor degree, all of which were unpunished, and that witnesses could not safely testify in the courts there unless the more active members were placed under restraint.

(Signed)   U. S. GRANT.

Executive Mansion, April 19, 1872.

———◦◦◦———

[From the *Nation*, March 28, 1872.]

"Seven years have gone over us since the close of the war, and, instead of occupying this precious season with endeavors to re-establish prosperity, and to

sow the seeds of a peace, which in another genera-
tion, would ripen into good will and forgetfulness,
we have averted our eyes from the whole problem,
refused to listen to the complaints of men whose
hands we have tied, and have fallen back upon the
lazy belief that in some way this great country is
bound to go through. The unconscious syllogism
working in the indolent Northern mind seems to be:
'Things are no doubt very bad — how bad, we
have 'n't the time, or the inclination to ascertain.
Examination of such unpleasant matters, if a duty at
all, is a disagreeable one. After all, the rebels have
made their own bed, and they must lie in it.' Perhaps their sufferings are only the just punishment of
their crimes. . . . . But let us make up our minds
one way or the other — do we or do we not propose
further to punish the rebel states for their rebellion?
If we do, let us at once proceed to devise some intelligent means for that purpose. *If we do not, let us
make haste to protect society* [at the South] *from the
ravages of ignorance and rapacity, or give society* [at
the South] *the means to protect itself.*"

[From *Harper's Weekly*, April 20, 1872.]

"The great question in this quarter [the South] is
the problem of reconstruction, and I am inclined to
think that it is *the most important national question.*

It is hardly worth our time, at this late day, to ask whether the reconstruction laws are the wisest that could have been devised. They are laws, and have been sufficiently tested to convince us that *their faithful administration will lead to the results anticipated* by those who were instrumental in their enactment. I think it better, therefore, *to adhere to the original plan, than to start off upon some other theory, that may lead us into* NEW DIFFICULTIES, AND POSSIBLY INTO MOST DISASTROUS CONFUSION." — General James Longstreet to Senator W. P. Kellogg.

HOW TO EXTIRPATE KU–KLUXISM FROM THE SOUTH.

A Preliminary Word.

Although the Northern People have good cause for congratulating themselves on their good fortune in solving many of the more important and urgent of the very complicated social and political problems which the exigencies of the national life have, during the last decade, forced upon their attention; yet their very laudable and patriotic efforts to establish an unanimity of sentiment and sympathies in national matters between the North and the South have not, so far, been crowned with complete or deserved success. On the contrary, it would seem that at no former period in the history of the nation, was there

so little good feeling between these two great sections
as at this very moment. Judging from current events
that are manifest to all, mutual enmity, deep and vin-
dictive, is the one great and ever present motive that
influences, directs, and altogether controls their public intercourse,—which renders both sections unwil-
ling or unable to prevent the intrusion of sectional
jealousies and party prejudices into discussions
even of the most momentous public questions.
That this is a most unsatisfactory state of affairs,
no one will deny; and every good citizen, whether
of the North or of the South, must earnestly desire
that a more fraternal disposition should animate
them when dealing with national matters, in order
hat harmonic political, industrial, and commercial relations may, as speedily as possible, be established between them.   But, How to bring about this
greatly to be desired consummation? is a question
which, though continually discussed during the
last ten years, is to-day unsolved, and is, therefore,
an open question, still.   Of course, there is ample
room for any amount of honest difference of opinion
in regard to the most practicable or desirable man-
ner of solving it ; so that it is a most prolific source
of apparently endless speculation.   Nevertheless, it
is good to speculate on it.   In fact, the more it is discussed, the better.   The continuance of the present
disgraceful state of affairs (vide President's Message)

at the South must very seriously reflect upon the intelligence, to say nothing of the patriotism, of the Northern People, as the dominent party in this great controversy, and tend to bring discredit upon the institutions of the country, generally, with multitudes of people in the Old World. The more it is discussed in all its bearings, the sooner the mass of the people will realize this, and perceive the practical necessity, to all the best interests of the whole country, of terminating the present discreditable state of affairs at the South. And in the meantime, nothing is lost to the general result, though innumerable plans for its solution be offered, and upon examination, should fail to prove acceptable to the public ; for every rejected plan will contribute something towards hastening the production of the one which will ultimately prove the successful one. Therefore, let every one, who feels inclined to do so, keep "pegging away" at it after his own fashion. In this view, one thing, however, is to be noted, viz., the economic interests involved, rather than the political and sentimental aspects of the question, should receive prominence. The latter have obtained their full share of public attention, while the former have very generally been ignored.

This unsettled state of the question is our excuse for offering the following suggestions in the matter.

But, first of all, it is to be observed that in view of

the fact, that the present phase of the difficulty between the North and the South has already continued
for eight long and dreary years, whereas half that
time sufficed in which to annihilate the whole of rebel
armies, the conclusion is inevitable that the Northern
People are making some very serious mistake in con-
ducting their case in its present form; and consequently, that they must make some radical change in
their Southern policy, before they can hope to gain
their cause at the South.

Now we shall assume (it is unnecessary to trouble
the reader with arguments in the matter, for if he feels
inclined to reject these our conclusions, he would not
be likely to pay any serious attention to our premises
for them, were they presented) the following points:—

(1.) That the fatal mistake of the Northern People in their Southern policy since the dispersion of
the rebel armies, has been their reliance upon United
States Marshals and United States soldiers, almost
exclusively, to represent them at the South ; (2.) that
their true course to pursue towards the South is to
colonize it with at least One Hundred Thousand
(100,000) intelligent, respectable, and industrious
Northern Working Men ; (3.) that, inasmuch as the
Federal Government found no very great difficulty,
any time during the late war, in inducing a million
of Northern men to exchange the security, peace, and
enjoyment of their homes for the dangers and priva-

tions of prolonged active warfare in the face of a
determined and powerful enemy at the South and to
remain there year after year, until the overthrow of
their antagonists left them free to return to their
homes,— there are 100,000 of those same men who
would gladly return South now with the implements
of peace in their hands, to make their homes there,
provided they had the means to enable them to do
so ; (4.) that One Thousand (1000) Dollars per man
would be all sufficient to establish them comfortably
there ; (5.) that the required funds would readily
enough be forthcoming, were the proper parties to
ask the public for them ; and (6.) that the proper
parties to collect the required funds, and to select
the proposed colonists, and superintend the suggested
undertaking, generally, are the GRAND ARMY
OF THE REPUBLIC, and the various WORKING
MEN'S SOCIETIES throughout the North. Consequently, in this view, the only question for consideration is, How are the societies above named to
secure the necessary funds, namely, One Hundred
Million Dollars? for the projected undertaking.

OUR SOLUTION OF THE PROBLEM:

1. Let every Post of the G. A. R., and every
Working Man's Society form itself into a Local
Committee to assist in collecting One Hundred Mil-
lion Dollars for the purpose of Colonizing the South

with One Hundred Thousand respectable and industrious Northern men.

2. Let the said Committee appoint such persons as it shall deem proper, to collect for the said Colonizing Fund: the Committee being, of course, responsible to the general public in the matter.

3. Let every such collector be supplied by the Committee with a quantity of *Numbered Tickets* for him to dispose of in his own way, at the rate of Ten (10) cents per each Ticket; the proceeds of such sales to be turned over to the Committee, at least once a week.

4. On a given day of each and every week, let Twenty-five (25) per centum of the gross sum so collected during the week next preceding the said day, be by lot distributed by the Committee among a due proportion of the then holders of its tickets, each distribution canceling all the then outstanding non-prize-drawing tickets of the distributing Committee.

5. Let the remaining Seventy-five (75) per centum be retained by the Committee, until by weekly accruments, it shall amount to the sum, say, for instance, of Fifty Thousand Dollars ($50,000); which sum the Committee shall then divide into Fifty equal parts of $1000 each, which parts it shall immediately distribute by lot among a proper proportion of such persons, as the said Committee shall previously have determined to be eligible for membership in a co-

operative company for the purpose of colonizing the South. And

6. Let the *Holders* of the *Successful Numbers* at once associate themselves together as a CO-OPERATIVE COMPANY OF COLONISTS FOR THE SOUTH, which organization being completed, the Committee to deposit, to the credit of said Company, the said $50,000 with some responsible Banker, which shall constitute such banker the Legal Treasurer of the said Company, and, as such, he shall hold its funds subject to the order only of its duly appointed officers, for the payment of the legitimate expenses of the Company.*

Here, then, briefly stated, are some general suggestions in the matter, which would seem to afford the basis of a practical plan for procuring the funds required for the project of Colonizing the South with 100,000 Northern men of the right stamp, and provide for the efficient superintendence generally of such an undertaking. But let us look at them a little closer.

---

* Possibly the reader, while not disposed to think unfavorable of the other features of this plan, will object to the proposed mode of soliciting the required funds, and deem it more appropriate to appeal to Congress for them. The writer, however, is of opinion, that were Congress even ready to grant the whole amount in question for the mere asking, nevertheless it would not be desirable to accept it from Congress. To be effective the proposed movement must be a *bona fide* popular movement from first to last.

Obviously, according to 'clause 1,' the management of the whole affair, from first to last, would be placed in the hands of men who are every way competent to direct such a movement to a successful issue, and who would, in regard to it, start with the full and entire confidence of the general public in every section of the country: to 'clause 3,' its inauguration would be easy, simple, and inexpensive; imposing no preliminary expense upon the Local Committees, except the cost of printing a few tickets; neither would its successful prosecution make any inconvenient, or even noticable demand, on the time of the several collectors; so that, without expense or inconvenience to any one, it might, from its very inception, be secured a real, permanent, popular, and most efficient organization, which would go far to ensure its success among the general public: to 'clause 3,' its requirements would be adapted to popular convenience: to 'clause 4,' popular interest would be enlisted for its success: to 'clause 5,' favoritism in the distribution of the Company prizes would be effectually prevented; and every possible recipient of a share secured a fair chance for it and: to 'clause 6,' any squandering of the Company fund would be rendered very difficult, if not absolutely impossible, and the "Company" would, to begin with, have a recognized standing in the business community.

But, after all, the real test of the practicalness of

any plan for the purpose above indicated must be the facilities it would afford for procuring the required funds, for evidently nothing can be done in the matter without money. Money, and a very large amount of it, too, is the one thing needful, before the plan could take tangible shape even, much less the object involved be advanced a single step. Well then, What would be the result of the operation of the present plan in this respect? For an answer to this question, we must be content with an inference from the reasonable probabilities of the case. Now, what are the reasonable probabilities of the case? Let us see.

As a little examination of it will show, this plan endeavors to interest every class of the whole population of the country in its success. To this end, it bases its primary appeal upon purely economic and business principles. In return for a reasonable chance of receiving considerable more than a fair equivelent for his money, it asks 10 cents a week of the poor man who may desire to invest in it, and requires no more from the rich man ; but if the latter be of a charitable, philanthropic, patriotic, or generous disposition, it presents ample opportunities to him to exercise his disposition in its behalf to any extent he pleases. It would take care that all sums, whether great or small, or from whatever motive given, should go forth on the same peaceful and patriotic mission. Therefore, it is reasonable to conclude that these

motives would influence the wealthy to contribute
liberally towards the proposed movement, when it had
once taken palpable shape, and it is reasonable, also,
to assume that these contributions, together with
those from other causes, would, in the aggregate, equal
a regular weekly contribution of 10 cents from one
in every five of the entire population of any given
locality. Obviously, this number is altogether too low
to cover the reasonable probabilities in the case ; it
might be put as high as four in every five, without
going beyond them. But let us keep to the former
number. Now, this datum, applied to any community,
will give us a good trustworthy answer to our question. Let us, then, apply it, say to the City of New
York, for

EXAMPLE.

That city contains 1,000,000 inhabitants, and our
datum gives us 200,000 of those as contributing for
this cause 10 cents each regularly every week ; which
is $20,000 per week ; and that, minus 25 per cent.
(vide clause 4) gives $60,000 as the net monthly in-
come for this cause in that community alone. And
this sum is abundant to provide a colony of 60 respectable and industrious Northern men with every
thing necessary for their establishing themselves comfortably at the South. That is to say, if each of the
above stated number of the people of that city would
weekly place a sum of money, so utterly insignificant

that it is exceeded by the cost of a glass of soda water
or a cheap cigar, in the hands of men whom they all
know to be trustworthy and thoroughly competent for
the work, — these men could guarantee to return
them 25 per cent. of their contributions, and, with the
remainder, send out every month a new Company of
sixty picked Northern men as colonists to the South,
fully equiped, and furnished with sufficient capital to
ensure the success of the enterprise.

Now, to establish even one such colony in each
county in any given Southern State would, for all the
practical purposes of the case, be to colonize that entire State. Well, then, the State of South Carolina, for
instance, contains 30 counties ; what an easy thing,
therefore, it would be for New York City alone, to
colonize, with men of its own choice, the whole State
of South Carolina in the brief space of about two
years. That is what one single Northern community*
could do for an entire Southern State, without put-
ting any one of its citizens to the slightest inconvenience in the matter. Now, extend the operations
of this plan, until they should embrace every Northern
community, which could be easily done, and in how
little time the whole South would be colonized with

---

*Or, if we take four in five as the probable proportion of con-
tributers in any given population, the State of Massachusetts
could, in this way, raise funds enough within her own limits,
in about *Three Months*, to colonize the whole State of South
Carolina.

picked men from the ranks of the industrial classes of the North. Reader, think it over. And then consider that the Northern People have been "reconstructing" the South for the last eight years, at an immense expenditure of money, without reconciling the first Southern state, city, town, or even village, to their views on public matters.

But, all purely patriotic considerations aside, the success of this plan would, in a mere speculative and economic point of view, prove highly beneficial to the industrial and business interests of the North. Its operations, if extended to anything like National proportions, would necessarily open a vast field for utilizing the immense mass of well disposed and intelligent, but adventurous young energy now wandering aimless about the North; they would provide acceptable and remunerative employment, at the South, for multitudes of Northern working people who find it impossible to secure the means of a decent support for themselves and their families in their present abodes. For, while individual Northern enterprise in that direction is not just now advisable, yet thoughout the whole civilized world, there is not another so favorable an opening for co operative Northern enterprise, if it be united, systematic, and of a legitimate character, as the South, in its present condition, offers to it. Every associated enterprise, such as this plan suggests, if judiciously located and prop-

erly managed for developing the natural resources of
the South, instead of (as some have done) plunging
into mad attempts at competition with great Northern
industries, would handsomely compensate the laborer
for his work, besides, after the first year, paying cent-
per-cent. per annum on every dollar of capital invested
in it. Once settled at the South, the colonists, amidst
congenial social surroundings that this plan would
secure to him, could not, with a tithe of the industry,
fail to secure an ample competency for themselves
and their dependents, without that incessant toil
which, for even a scanty and pecarious support, the
North exacts from every person who depends solely
upon manual labor.for their livelihood within its great
centers of population. Thus they would materially
benefit themselves in all the relations of life, and, at
the same time, leave a freer field to, and open a new
market for, the industry of those of their fraternity
who are established at the North. It would, also,
give a new and lasting impetus to legitimate business
of all kinds throughout the whole country. Therefore, leaving Southern interests and political considerations out of the question altogether, this plan de-
serves the serious attention of the Working men and
the Business men of the North.

Of course, it is not at all impossible that a careless,
indifferent, or prejudiced reader may regard it in another light. To such, it may, perhaps, appear an

impractical and Utopian method of dealing with the
great problem in question, and, consequently, unde-
serving of any consideration from practical men. The
careful and unprejudiced reader, however, who really
understands the very critical state in which the political, the commercial, and the industrial affairs of the
whole country are placed, by reason of the disorgan-
ized and discontented condition of Southern society,
and fully appreciates the great difficulties in the way
of practical and efficient legislation, whether local or
National, upon the subject — thus comprehending the
real character of the numerous and diverse elements
involved in this Reconstruction problem — will, at
once, perceive that the plan, here briefly outlined,
does not present a single impracticable or fanciful
feature. But that, on the contrary, it is a plain, simple, every-day, working plan, which, in fact, it is. It
takes things just as it finds them. It accepts the
materials that are presented to it, and, as it were,
prepared expressly for its purpose. Thus, the men
are all ready, were the order given, to embark upon
this projected Southern mission ; the money for it is,
as we have seen, all ready — aye, in sober truth, it is
lying "round loose" for the hand of the proper persons to gather it up — and machinery, so perfectly
adapted for collecting this money, and, also, for se-
lecting the right men for this mission, that it would
be impossible to conceive of any more appropriate

for those purposes, is all ready. And, further, the
men who control this machinery have, ere this, risked
their lives, time and again, in this identical cause, to
which they are now asked only to devote occasionally
nothing more than a few of their leisure hours, in order
that they may secure for themselves and their children
after them, the fruits of their previous sacrifices and
exertions in the cause. Is there anything very visionary in supposing that these men might set the
machinery in motion in the desired direction, and
that a generous and patriotic public would sustain
them in the matter? If this be visionary, then the
whole Northern People are now, and have, for the
last twelve years, been the most visionary of vision-
ists in their Southern Policy.

———oo⚬⚬oo———

" When the Senate of the United States met on the 5th
December 1860, for the second session of the XXXVIth
Congress, there was a long list of absentees from the
Southern States. Senators Toombs of Georgia, Clay of
Alabama, Slidell and Benjamin of Louisiana, Mason of
Virginia, Mallory of Florida, Johnson and Sebastian of
Arkansas and both the South Carolina Senators were at
home working up the excitement that swept over their
section of the country and resulted in the several ordi-
nances of secession. Most of these absent Senators sub-
sequently appeared and took their seats. The South
Carolina members did not. No communication, so far as
appears from the record in the Globe, was ever received
from either. They merely neglected to appear. On the

21st of January 1861, Senators Yulee and Mallory of
Florida, Clay and Fitzpatrick of Alabama and Davis of
Mississippi took formal leave of the Senate in carefully
prepared speeches. Thus was made the first breach in the
representation of the States of the Union in the Senate,
that was but yesterday fully repaired. One by one the
States came back, but the delay in the readmission of some
of them continued so long that meanwhile others failed to
be represented. At last the roll is once more completed.
Thirty-seven States are represented by seventy-four Senators. There have been vacant seats for almost twelve
years, — ever since the adjournment of the first session of
the XXXVIth Congress, — several months before the
election of Abraham Lincoln." — The *Advertiser*, April
25th.

Here we have a compendious epitome of one of the most
important chapters in all history. So then, at long
length, the governmental machinery of the Nation is
once more complete, and in running order. But one
section of it don't work quite smoothly yet; and so the
entire structure is continually exposed to serious danger.

In another Boston daily, the *Herald*, April 29, we read:

" Attorney General Williams has replied to a resolution
of the House, asking details of the measures taken for the
enforcement of the Ku-Klux act. He gives little encourage-
ment to those who want to keep the South under martial law.
. . . . He believes that with an influx of emigrants it
could not be long before all lawlessness and violence grow-
ing out of political differences, radical antagonisms, and
social distinctions, would be a thing of the past."

Made in the USA
Las Vegas, NV
06 January 2022